# HIP-HOP

Alicia Keys
Ashanti
Beyoncé
Black Eyed Peas
Busta Rhymes
Chris Brown
Christina Aguilera
Ciara
Cypress Hill
Daddy Yankee
DMX
Don Omar
Dr. Dre
Eminem
Fat Joe
50 Cent
The Game
Hip-Hop: A Short History
Hip-Hop Around the World
Ice Cube
Ivy Queen
Jay-Z
Jennifer Lopez
Juelz Santana
Kanye West

Lil Wayne
LL Cool J
Lloyd Banks
Ludacris
Mariah Carey
Mary J. Blige
Missy Elliot
Nas
Nelly
Notorious B.I.G.
OutKast
Pharrell Williams
Pitbull
Queen Latifah
Reverend Run (of Run DMC)
Sean "Diddy" Combs
Snoop Dogg
T.I.
Tupac
Usher
Will Smith
Wu-Tang Clan
Xzibit
Young Jeezy
Yung Joc

In the world of music and one-hit wonders, Cypress Hill is unique. While most groups come and go in a blink, Cypress Hill have been together making music and making history for almost twenty years.

# Hip-Hop

# Cypress Hill

MaryJo Lemmens

Mason Crest Publishers

Cypress Hill

Produced by Harding House Publishing Service, Inc., 201 Harding Avenue, Vestal, NY 13850.

MASON CREST PUBLISHERS INC.
370 Reed Road
Broomall, Pennsylvania 19008
(866)MCP-BOOK (toll free)
www.masoncrest.com

Printed in the United States of America

First Printing

9 8 7 6 5 4 3 2 1

Library of Congress Cataloging-in-Publication Data

Lemmens, MaryJo.
  Cypress Hill / Mary Jo Lemmens.
      p. cm. — (Hip-hop)
  Includes bibliographical references and index.
  ISBN 978-1-4222-0287-6
  ISBN: 978-1-4222-0077-3 (series)
  1. Cypress Hill (Musical group)—Juvenile literature.  2. Rap musicians—United States—Biography—Juvenile literature.  I. Title.
  ML3930.C975L46 2008
  782.421649092'2—dc22
  [B]
                              2007031167

Publisher's notes:
• All quotations in this book come from original sources and contain the spelling and grammatical inconsistencies of the original text.

• The Web sites mentioned in this book were active at the time of publication. The publisher is not responsible for Web sites that have changed their addresses or discontinued operation since the date of publication. The publisher will review and update the Web site addresses each time the book is reprinted.

DISCLAIMER: The following story has been thoroughly researched, and to the best of our knowledge, represents a true story. While every possible effort has been made to ensure accuracy, the publisher will not assume liability for damages caused by inaccuracies in the data, and makes no warranty on the accuracy of the information contained herein. This story has not been authorized nor endorsed by Cypress Hill.

# Contents

# Hip-Hop Time Line

1976 Grandmaster Flash and the Furious Five emerge as one of the first battlers and freestylers.

1984 The track "Roxanne Roxanne" sparks the first diss war.

1970s DJ Kool Herc pioneers the use of breaks, isolations, and repeats using two turn-tables.

1982 Afrika Bambaataa tours Europe in another hip-hop first.

1988 Hip-hop record sales reach 100 million annually.

1970s Grafitti artist Vic begins tagging on New York subways.

1980 Rapper Kurtis Blow sells a million records and makes the first nationwide TV appearance for a hip-hop artist.

1985 The film *Krush Groove*, about the rise of Def Jam Records, is released.

## 1970        1980

1970s The central elements of the hip-hop culture begin to emerge in the Bronx, New York City.

1983 Ice-T releases his first singles, marking the earliest examples of gangsta rap.

1986 Run DMC cover Aerosmith's "Walk this Way" and appear on the cover of *Rolling Stone*.

1979 "Rapper's Delight," by The Sugarhill Gang, goes gold.

1984 *Graffitti Rock*, the first hip-hop television program, premieres.

1974 Afrika Bambaataa organizes the Universal Zulu Nation.

1981 Grandmaster Flash and the Furious Five release *Adventures on the Wheels of Steel*.

1988 MTV premieres *Yo! MTV Raps*.

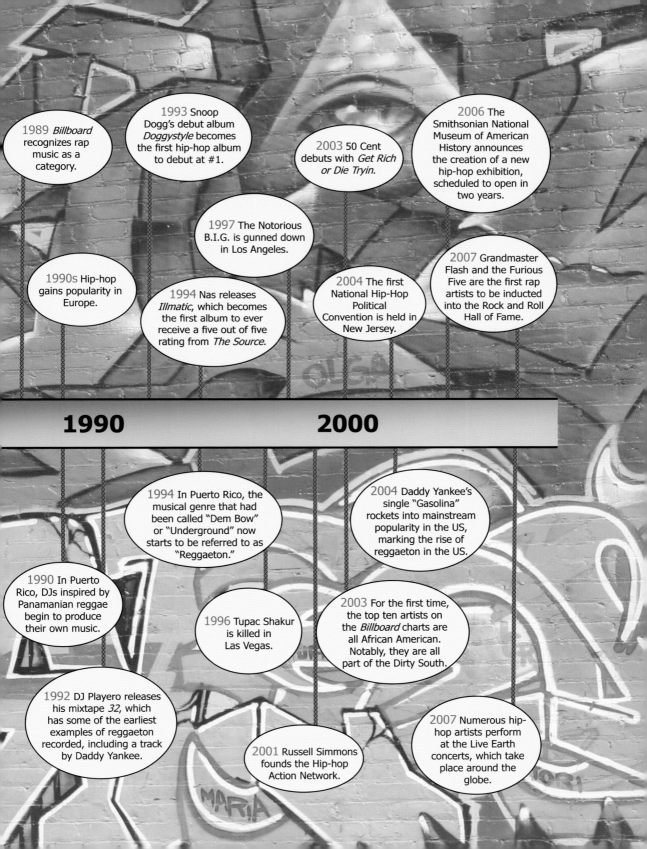

1989 *Billboard* recognizes rap music as a category.

1993 Snoop Dogg's debut album *Doggystyle* becomes the first hip-hop album to debut at #1.

2003 50 Cent debuts with *Get Rich or Die Tryin.*

2006 The Smithsonian National Museum of American History announces the creation of a new hip-hop exhibition, scheduled to open in two years.

1997 The Notorious B.I.G. is gunned down in Los Angeles.

2007 Grandmaster Flash and the Furious Five are the first rap artists to be inducted into the Rock and Roll Hall of Fame.

1990s Hip-hop gains popularity in Europe.

1994 Nas releases *Illmatic*, which becomes the first album to ever receive a five out of five rating from *The Source*.

2004 The first National Hip-Hop Political Convention is held in New Jersey.

# 1990

# 2000

1994 In Puerto Rico, the musical genre that had been called "Dem Bow" or "Underground" now starts to be referred to as "Reggaeton."

2004 Daddy Yankee's single "Gasolina" rockets into mainstream popularity in the US, marking the rise of reggaeton in the US.

1990 In Puerto Rico, DJs inspired by Panamanian reggae begin to produce their own music.

1996 Tupac Shakur is killed in Las Vegas.

2003 For the first time, the top ten artists on the *Billboard* charts are all African American. Notably, they are all part of the Dirty South.

1992 DJ Playero releases his mixtape *32*, which has some of the earliest examples of reggaeton recorded, including a track by Daddy Yankee.

2001 Russell Simmons founds the Hip-hop Action Network.

2007 Numerous hip-hop artists perform at the Live Earth concerts, which take place around the globe.

When hip-hop began, it was all about the DJ and a couple of turntables. But, as the genre evolved, technology began to replace much of what the DJ did. Still, the purpose of hip-hop was the same—to entertain the audience.

# A Hip-Hop History

DJ Muggs' haunting loops punctuate the deep bass rhythms of "I Ain't Goin' Out Like That." B-Real's high-pitched vocals pierce the psychedelic air, lending a strange steadiness to DJ Muggs' sweeping *samples*. The repetition becomes mesmerizing; you're getting pulled in. Suddenly, Sen Dog explodes into the song, shouting out the chorus. His aggressive vocals send a shudder through the music. Behind it all, Eric Bobo handles the beat, driving the song down its rhythmic path. Together, these four men make up Cypress Hill, one of the most successful rap groups of our time.

For nearly two decades, Cypress Hill has created music that is entertaining, cutting edge, and controversial. Hailing from California, the group began in the late 1980s and earned its first widespread success in the early 1990s. Cypress Hill is unique in hip-hop because of the way the group blends different styles into its music. The group is never afraid to experiment. At various times, they have incorporated rock, *punk*, *funk*, heavy metal, and alternative styles into their songs. At the core, however, Cypress Hill is hip-hop.

## Where It All Began

Hip-hop (also called rap) is the harsh music of the inner city and the hopeful expression of people's dreams. This music clawed its way out of the ghetto, overcame color lines and class barriers, and became some of the most popular music on earth. Today, millions of people around the world are hip-hop fans. People love it for its blood-pumping beats and real-world lyrics. It's music that grabs you and doesn't let go. When you listen to hip-hop, you want to jump to it, rap with it, throw your fist up and be defiant. It's alive and real, and it moves your soul. At its best, the music raises you up, entertains you, and inspires you. It allows you to escape and, for a moment, be something different.

The hip-hop music of today has come a long way from its roots. Now hip-hop is all over the radio. It blares from car windows on every street in America. It's downloaded onto millions of iPods, played in millions of homes, and featured in countless commercials and movie soundtracks. But just a few decades ago, hip-hop existed only in the heart of America's toughest neighborhoods. It all began in the Bronx, a region of New York City, in the early 1970s. At that time, the Bronx, like many urban areas around America, experienced rapid decline as people moved to suburbs and new types of urban planning changed neighborhoods.

The Bronx in the 1970s had a lot of problems. Some of the biggest were ill-conceived construction projects that destroyed many neighborhoods and sent others into a tailspin of decline. One of these projects was the Cross-Bronx Expressway, a huge highway that cut across the city, separating and leveling neighborhoods in its path. Another was the building of huge blocks of public housing. They were meant to provide quality housing for low-income people. Instead they became areas of concentrated poverty and crime and earned the infamous nickname: "the projects."

By the seventies, the people with enough money to do so had fled the changing Bronx neighborhoods. The poorest residents, most of whom were African American or Latino, were

You can take the subway right to hip-hop's birthplace. Hip-hop was born in the Bronx section of New York City, in the heavily African American and Latino neighborhoods. The people might have not had much money, but they knew how to party.

left behind to face falling property values, declining schools, and increasing crime. Arson plagued the borough, especially on the south side, and gave birth to the famous phrase "The Bronx is burning." It was a harsh world, marred by poverty, crime, and hopelessness. Young people searched for meaning, hope, and a way to express themselves. They wanted recognition and respect, but for poor black and Latino kids in the Bronx, recognition and respect were hard to come by.

The 1970s were a rough time in the Bronx. Poverty, frustration, and a sense of hopelessness led to high crime rates. Crimes like arson were commonplace in the borough.

# The Ghetto Gives Birth

In the 1970s Bronx communities, people didn't have much, but they could still have fun. Music and dancing were a great way for people to let loose, forget about their problems, and raise their spirits. Clubs, block parties, and impromptu gatherings in parks—complete with DJs and dancing—were hugely popular. DJs could set up equipment and get a party started virtually anywhere, anytime. They didn't even need an electrical outlet to power their equipment. No place to plug in? No problem. The DJ just hotwired a streetlight to juice his speakers and amps. Technically, you were supposed to apply for a permit to have a party on a block or in a park, and stealing electricity from the city certainly wasn't legal, but the cops often looked the other way and avoided the toughest neighborhoods.

So when the opportunity arose, people partied. The DJs were the life of those parties, spinning the tunes that kept everyone dancing. Funk and disco were the popular music of the era, and DJs kept the dance tunes playing, one after the other. But DJs soon discovered they could do more than just pop a record on a turntable and let it play. The best DJs were *innovators* who experimented with the music, rallied the crowd, and gave the partygoers a show. The newest innovation would be hip-hop.

Hip-hop began when DJs (DJ Kool Herc is usually given the credit) introduced a Jamaican style of *cutting* and mixing music into their shows. The technique used two turntables, each with a record. Sometimes they were two copies of the same record. Sometimes they were two different records. The DJ isolated the breaks (or beat-driven sections of the songs) and mixed back and forth between the two records. The technique allowed a DJ to take one small sample of a song (maybe just fifteen seconds) and extend it and mix it into something different. The sampling and mixing got more innovative and complex, becoming its own art form that created a completely new sound in music.

Soon the DJs added another element to their shows. They began working the microphone as well as the turntable. As the music pumped, some DJs emceed, entertaining the crowd with jokes, stories, banter, boasts, or anything that came to mind. Emceeing became bigger and more complex, and broke away from DJing into an independent part of the show. Now there were DJs and MCs. The DJs spun the music, and the MCs entertained the crowd by speaking in rhythms and rhymes. The style soon had its own name: rapping. Hip-hop was born.

## Graffiti Crews and B-Boys

Music is the most well-known part of hip-hop culture, but hip-hop isn't just about music. Today hip-hop culture has its own styles of dance, art, fashion, and even language. In the 1970s, these elements were also developing alongside the music. Graffiti, or tagging, inspired hip-hop's visual art styles. While many people think that graffiti is just a form of vandalism, others feel that graffiti is part of a whole underground movement of expression, rebellion, and claiming public space that, at its best, becomes an art.

Tagging began simply as a way to say, "I was here." In the beginning, it was just a name or number scrawled on a subway car or city bus. But tagging caught on, and soon just making your mark wasn't enough. Taggings got bigger and more elaborate. Taggers used spray paint to make their works larger and accomplish them faster (they wanted to leave their mark, but they didn't want to get caught in the act), and sometimes they worked in crews. Some taggers became artists, making graffiti that was colorful, complex, and thought provoking. The artistic styles they developed, like "block," "bubble," and "wildstyle," became strong visual influences on hip-hop culture, and they are still an important part of hip-hop today.

Hip-hop is about more than music. Art in the form of graffiti also plays a role in the hip-hop culture, though some might question whether it is really art or just vandalism. What began as tagging, letting people know one "was here," became more daring and more elaborate.

The group Soul Assassins, a collective of hip-hop musicians (including Cypress Hill) and graphic artists, is just one example of how the musical and visual arts of hip-hop remain closely linked. Today, you will see graffiti-inspired designs not just on walls, but on T-shirts, posters, advertisements, and all different forms of graphic art.

While sampling, rapping, and graffiti developed, a new dance form made its own mark on hip-hop culture. DJs and MCs cranked the music, graffiti crews put hip-hop's mark on

One of the goals of hip-hop has always been to get people up and dancing. Some dancers took the challenge further, making moves that can cause viewers to get hurt. Before long, break-dancers were trying to see who could send their bodies into the most complex contortions.

the streets, and b-boys (also called break-dancers) got down on the dance floor. Like their musical and artistic counterparts, the first b-boys were great innovators. They took dancing to a whole new physical level by combining complex footwork with full-body moves, gymnastics, and martial-arts techniques. What resulted was a highly improvisational, rhythmic, and acrobatic dance form that requires incredible skill, strength, and power.

## A Hip-Hop Attitude

Like everyone else in the world, poor black and Latino youths in the Bronx wanted recognition and respect—two things that were hard to come by in their world. Getting a good education, landing a great job, and working hard to acquire wealth and status have always been promoted as the surest road to respect and success in the United States. But in the 1970s, there were a lot of roadblocks to success for black, Latino, and other minority young people on this traditional path. The effects of decades of segregationist policies, widespread and persistent poverty, and inadequate schools virtually guaranteed that most minority kids would never make it down that hard road to accomplishment. To the kids of the Bronx, the reality that the "American dream" had little room for them was plain to see, and they looked for other ways to earn the recognition and respect that wealthy, white America denied them.

The music, dance, and art of the developing hip-hop culture were a way young people could earn respect and status in their communities. Hip-hop's many forms of expression became forms of competition: who could tag the most places, who could mix the best music, who could spit the best rhymes, who could break down with the best moves. Today we think of gangs battling with guns, but in the 1970s, gangs of young people, mostly young men, used music, art, and dance to battle for turf and respect. That's not to say that DJing, MCing, tagging, and breakdancing replaced violence in the streets. They certainly did not, and sometimes a score on the stage or dance floor might even be settled with violence later on. But this new art of the ghetto did give young people a way to express themselves and something to take pride in, and the best DJs, MCs, b-boys, b-girls, and graffiti artists earned respect and followers.

Hip-hop was born in the Bronx, but it didn't stay there for long. It spread throughout New York City, then to other cities. Soon it reached all the way across the country. People loved hip-hop because it wasn't just music; hip-hop was a whole attitude and way of life—an in-your-face challenge to the **mainstream**. And the best thing about it was that you didn't have to be rich or have any special training to do it. Anyone with a thought, a voice, and a rhyme could rap. Anyone with a can of paint and a name could tag. Anyone with the guts to try could b-boy. There were no rules holding you back and no right way to do things. It was all experimentation and individuality. In an interview with latinrapper.com, Cypress Hill's Sen Dog remembered what it was like in hip-hop's early days:

> *"You know when we first started in Hip Hop, me and [my brother] were the first two cats on our street into it, things just had a really Hip Hop attitude back then. We lived the life, we lived the culture, we breakdanced, we pop locked, rapped at parties. . . . Anybody can live Hip Hop."*

As hip-hop spread throughout the country, each artist and region contributed something new to the music and culture. Regional styles like East Coast and West Coast developed, and rivalries began. East Coast artists were more successful and popular through the1980s, but at the end of the decade West Coast artists like Cypress Hill rose up.

Sen Dog, B-Real, DJ Muggs, and Eric Bobo were all just kids when hip-hop started in the Bronx and migrated to the tough neighborhoods of other American cities. By the late 1980s, however, they were leaving their teenage years behind. Hip-hop music was leaving its youth behind as well. The departure of its youth was also, in a way, a departure of innocence as a new style of hip-hop called "gangsta rap" developed. It started in Philadelphia, but quickly moved to the West Coast and became a defining style of that region's music. That's when Cypress Hill emerged on the hip-hop scene. By the mid-1990s, West Coast rap dominated the hip-hop industry, and Cypress Hill was one of the West Coast's biggest names.

Though hip-hop was born on the East Coast, it was too big to be held to one region. It eventually made its way across the country, where it landed in the Los Angeles area. There, Cypress Hill began their decades-long career.

# The MCs and the Mixmaster

Cypress Hill's story begins in South Gate, California, in the mid-1980s. South Gate, a city in Los Angeles County, wasn't as dangerous as some of the nearby cities, like **notorious** Compton, but it had its risky neighborhoods. In the rougher areas, drug-dealing, gun-toting gangs roamed the streets and battled over turf. There were plenty of opportunities for a young person to get into trouble, and the members of Cypress Hill got into their fair share.

## B-Real

One of those young kids was a boy named Louis Freese. He was the son of a strict Mexican father and a Cuban mother. Back in Cuba, Louis's mother had been opposed to Fidel Castro, the revolutionary leader who seized power and introduced communist policies to the island and its government. Her political activities landed her in prison. She would never accept Castro's rule, and after escaping prison, she fled as a refugee to the United States, where she met her husband and started a family.

Louis was born on June 2, 1970. One day he would become B-Real, the lead rapper of Cypress Hill. In 1984, however, he was just fourteen years old and getting his first taste of rap music. Unfortunately for Louis, he was getting his fill of other less-constructive pastimes as well.

On his Web site, Louis describes both of his parents as "hustlers," doing what they needed to do to get by. According to Louis, his father was involved in gang activities. But both parents wanted their children to do better and tried to keep them out of trouble. While Louis was still young, he and his sister moved to South Gate with their mother. The seeds of rebellion, however, had already been planted. On his Web site, Louis says staying out of trouble would have been almost impossible:

*"My father and I didn't get along as I was growing up, as he was trying to prevent me from taking the same path that my brothers did. It was all around me, though, and nothing he could have done would have prevented the choices that I made growing up."*

One of those choices was to quit high school and join a gang. While still in his early teens, Louis met Senen Reyes. Meeting Sen started a whole new chapter in Louis's life. Soon he would see two doors before him. Behind each door lay a different path. One path led to music and self-expression, and one led to drugs, gangs, and self-destruction. Sen was five years older than Louis, and he already had his foot in each door.

## Senen Reyes

Probably one of the things that led Louis to Sen was his Cuban background. Like Louis's mother, Senen Reyes was born in Cuba. He had spent his childhood on the island, and was already a young teen when his family immigrated to the United States. The family spent some time in Miami, Florida, and New Jersey before eventually making their way to South Gate, California.

After moving to South Gate, Sen started running with the Bloods. The Bloods were a black gang that was very active in South Central Los Angeles. Gangs often formed along racial and *ethnic* lines, and Latinos didn't usually join the Bloods—although there wasn't any rule against it. Gang membership was about loyalty, not rules, but race usually played a big part in determining loyalties and who gang members would trust. So historically, Latino youths joined Latino gangs, black youths joined black gangs, white youths joined white gangs, and so on. But Sen was of Afro-Cuban heritage, which is perhaps one of the reasons he ran with the Bloods, a mostly black gang.

Gang membership, however, wasn't Sen's only interest. He was also into music. It was the early 1980s; hip-hop was big on the East Coast and beginning to spread around the country. Sen and his younger brother, Ulpiano (who would become better known as Mellow Man Ace), liked to break dance, pop lock (another dance style), write rhymes, and rap. Hip-hop was only just beginning to catch on in California, and their skills made the brothers big in the neighborhood. They eventually joined up with a DJ named Julio 6. Together the three men formed a crew called DVX, which stood for Devastating Vocal Xcellence.

Sen had a lot of respect on the street, and lots of guys wanted to run with him. It was 1984 when Sen's younger brother, Mellow Man, first rapped to Louis Freese. The experience made a big impression on Louis. He'd always liked to write poetry, but he never thought of taking it off the page and into music. Now he was turned on to the new sound and wanted to rap as well. He began hanging with Sen, rapping and transforming into B-Real. But Sen was part of DVX, and Louis didn't quite fit into the crew. Then, in 1986, Julio 6 introduced Louis to Lawrence Muggerud, better known as DJ Mixmaster Muggs.

## DJ Muggs

Lawrence Muggerud, who would one day become DJ Muggs and the only non-Latino member of Cypress Hill, was born on January 28, 1968, in Queens, New York. Lawrence's family was of Italian American and Norwegian American heritage. A

When it came to the early days of hip-hop, DJ Muggs was different than most of the genre's pioneers: he is neither African American nor Latino. Still, he definitely has what it takes to be a major hip-hop star.

few years after Lawrence was born, hip-hop began to develop in New York's toughest neighborhoods. One day, Lawrence would become one of the most important and innovative of hip-hop's second generation of DJs.

Growing up, Lawrence loved music. He especially liked *blues* and rock, but he listened to all types of music, and eventually the developing sounds of hip-hop reached his ears. In 1982, he moved to Southern California, and at about sixteen years old, Lawrence began DJing. Shortly after, he got his first set of turntables. He became a mobile DJ, hooking up with different rappers. He formed a crew called 7A3, who released an album but didn't stay together long. In 1986, he met Sen and Louis.

Since Louis was DVX's odd man out, Louis and Muggs paired up. They wrote some songs and cut some *demo* tapes together. Louis clearly had a gift for lyrics, and Muggs had a gifted ear and a talent for creating unique sounds. They grabbed some attention, particularly Sen's. When Sen's brother, Mellow Man Ace, decided to leave DVX to pursue a solo career, Sen joined Louis and Muggs. They named themselves Cypress Hill after a street in their neighborhood, and one of the most influential rap groups of all time was born.

## Gang Life

It would still be a number of years, however, before Cypress Hill, hit the charts. In fact, it would be a while before Louis even fully committed himself to the group and their music. He was just a teenager, and he was still getting into trouble and spending more time in dangerous activities than constructive pastimes.

When Louis started hanging with Sen, he was introduced to the Bloods. He was Latino, but his friendship with Sen gave him an in with the black gang. At first he was just Sen's friend, but he liked the guys he was running with, and before long he too joined the gang.

As a member of the Bloods, Louis dealt drugs. He also witnessed shootings, had lots of close calls, and saw friends get killed. On his Web site, he relates one of the close calls that could have ended everything for him:

*"I remember one occasion where I was on the block with 5 or 6 of my homies, bouncing a basketball. The ball hit the curb and bounced away. As I bent down to pick it up, a car rolled by with a guy sitting on the window ledge, aiming his gun over the roof of the car. When I ducked is when he started shooting. He missed me and caught one of my homies in the ankle. This lifestyle does catch up with you though, and one time I was not so lucky."*

As Louis says, when you're a member of a gang, luck can only stick with you for so long. Most people say there are only two ways a gang member can end up: in jail or dead. Louis almost ended up the latter one day when he went for a drug run with a friend. He tells the story on his Web site:

*"We got to a corner and a car full of Crips pulled up. . . . One of the Crips had a rifle and let off 5 shots. The first one hit my homie in the forearm. The last one hit me. It felt like a Charlie horse. I didn't even realize what had happened or how bad it was until I turned the corner and stopped to look to see if they were still after us. The bullet had punctured my lung. My homies took me to the hospital where I would lay on a gurney for 2 hours before anyone helped me. The cops came in to question me, asking me who shot me. Eventually they told me that I probably deserved it and left."*

Louis did pull through, but the shooting didn't mark the end of his gang life. For a while he tried to turn things around by focusing more on making music and less on gang activities. After too many close calls, Sen was also leaving gang life behind. He became very committed to Cypress Hill and the group's demo efforts. But Louis was having a hard time leaving the gang. He got bored with the demos and figured he was never going to make money with music anyway, so he quit the group for a while to return to the Bloods. But Sen and Muggs were persistent. They believed in their music, and they believed in Louis. One day, they sat Louis down and asked him to come back to Cypress Hill and leave gang life for good.

To say that Louis Freese wasn't exactly a natural rapper would be an understatement. Sen and Muggs even threatened to take the mic away from him. But with hard work, Louis got his sound down and became B-Real.

# Gangsta Rap

Eventually, Muggs and Sen got Louis to see reason. He rejoined Cypress Hill, but his position in the group wasn't guaranteed. Louis was great with lyrics, but he wasn't the best rapper. Muggs and Sen weren't crazy about Louis's voice. They wanted him to experiment and come up with something better. In fact, they said that if he didn't develop a better rapping technique, he'd have to just write for Sen.

Louis didn't just want to be a writer. He wanted to be heard. He wanted to be on stage. He wanted to be an MC. He began trying different voices and techniques, looking for a unique sound that would do justice to Mugg's music and Sen's style. On his Web site, he tells the story of how he found B-Real's voice:

*"One day, I was just [messin'] around to the Real Estate beat which Mellow Man originally wrote to but I rewrote.*

*I was just messin' around to it, trying different voices and deliveries and I did an early version of the voice I use now. The guys were like 'Do that again.' I thought they were crazy. I said it was wack and I wasn't going to rap like that, and they told me to either rap like that or not rap at all. So, I gave it a chance so I could be a rapper in the group. It took me a while to develop it and to be able to carry it for complete songs and albums, and especially while performing, but I got the hang of it after a while and I started to like how it sounded over the stuff Muggs was producing."*

Louis worked on the style and found his voice—the high-pitched, nasally sound that would one day become famous in the rap world. His transition to B-Real was complete. The group got to work on their first album, which would be called simply *Cypress Hill*. It was released in 1991, and the group began touring with artists like Ice Cube, Naughty by Nature, and Scarface. The touring helped give them exposure and start forming a fan base.

## Hip-Hop's New Age

The early 1990s was a great time for Cypress Hill to hit the airwaves. Hip-hop had entered a new age, breaking through many social barriers and becoming popular with wider audiences. For a long time, hip-hop was only heard on urban radio and rap stations, but throughout the 1980s artists like the Sugarhill Gang, Run DMC, the Beastie Boys, and Public Enemy had helped hip-hop cross over to mainstream radio. Once the music of urban black and Latino youths, hip-hop was now crossing color lines and economic barriers. It was becoming a universal music and language for young people, a trend that would only increase throughout the decade and into the new millennium.

Hip-hop exploded in the 1990s, gaining ever-growing legions of fans. While the fan-base grew, a new style of hip-hop formed and helped push the music's popularity to even greater heights. That new form of hip-hop was called "gangsta rap." It had started in Philadelphia, but quickly moved to California, where it became one of the defining elements of West Coast rap. Cypress Hill would soon be one of gangsta rap's pioneers. With the release of their first album, Cypress

When hip-hop came to the West Coast, it changed. Gangsta rap dominated West Coast rap. Songs were filled with lyrics about guns, violence, drugs, and hateful behaviors. Those characteristics also became part of many artists' real lives as well.

Though gangsta rap, and Cypress Hill's music, was controversial, it was also extremely popular. It didn't take long for Cypress Hill to develop a devoted fan base. At the same time, though, the group also developed a less devoted base of parents and others who weren't so happy with their music.

Hill was on the cutting edge of this new musical style. The group's debut album was filled with controversial gangsta rap themes.

The first single from the album was "The Phunky Feel One." It didn't get a whole lot of airplay or attention at first. As Cypress Hill began touring, however, a song called "How I Could Just Kill a Man" from the album's B-side grabbed people's attention. The group hadn't expected the song, with its focus on violence, guns, and murder, to be accepted by the mainstream. Lyrics like "Didn't have to blast him but I did anyway, That young punk had to pay," shocked a lot of people, but didn't stop the song from getting MTV and radio airplay. It became the biggest hit on the album, helping to eventually propel the record to double-*platinum* sales.

Other songs, like "Pig," which is about a corrupt cop who goes to prison where he faces payback from people he arrested in the past, were even more controversial. Many of the songs, like "Stoned is the Way of the Walk," were openly supportive of marijuana use. Soon Cypress Hill was earning scores of fans who loved the group not just for their music and lyrics, but also for their beliefs. What made Cypress Hill popular with fans, however, also made the group unpopular with many parents and other opponents of gangsta rap. In fact, Cypress Hill would become almost as famous for their members' open use of marijuana and belief that pot should be legalized as they were for their music.

# Critical Acclaim and Controversy

Many people heard more in Cypress Hill's first album than just explosive themes, explicit lyrics, and profanity. Behind the shocking words they heard *innovative* music with real artistic value. In fact, *Rolling Stone* magazine called *Cypress Hill* "an album that is innovative and engaging in spite of its hard-core messages." The album would one day become, in the words of *All Music Guide*'s Steve Huey, "a sonic blueprint that would become one of the most widely copied in hip-hop."

Cypress Hill's debut album didn't just define them as gangsta rappers, it also put them on the Latin hip-hop map. For B-Real and Sen Dog, it was important that their Latino heritage be part of their music. Tracks like "Latin Lingo" and "Tres Equis" featured Spanish lyrics and showed the guys' commitment to their Latino roots. Cypress Hill was now on their way to becoming the most successful Latino rap group of all time. The group's debut album was still in the *Billboard* 200's top ten two years later when their second album *Black Sunday* was released.

Many musical artists have one hit single, or one hot album, and then are never heard from again. In many ways, it's the second album that proves whether an artist has what it takes for more than fifteen seconds of fame. With their second album, Cypress Hill showed their staying power. *Black Sunday* came out in 1993, and it went immediately to #1 on the *Billboard* 200. The single "Insane in the Brain" was heavily rock influenced, and it became a huge **crossover** hit. The song helped expand Cypress Hill's fan base beyond just the hardcore hip-hop crowd and cement their popularity in the music world. *Black Sunday* became the group's second double-platinum album in a row.

Riding high on their new success, Cypress Hill went out on the road. They toured with groups like House of Pain, Rage Against the Machine, and the Beastie Boys. Not all the news was good, though—they got an invitation to play on *Saturday Night Live*, only to be banned forever after their first appearance on the show. Their crime? Smoking pot and destroying their instruments on air. But if getting banned from *Saturday Night Live* was a low point of their performances at this time, then meeting Eric Bobo was the high.

# Eric Bobo Completes the Crew

Eric Bobo, a percussionist who was touring with the Beastie Boys in 1992, was the son of Puerto Rican parents. He was born on August 27, 1968, in New York but later moved to California. His father's name was William Correa, but he was better known as the cutting-edge Latin *jazz* musician Willie Bobo.

As a boy, Eric had the privilege of studying the music of the jazz greats up close. When he was still young, he began playing live with his dad, and that gave him the opportunity to work with some of the biggest Latin jazz artists of the time. He was also a child during hip-hop's earliest years, and he absorbed these sounds as well.

By the time Eric was in his late teens, he was a versatile percussionist, knowledgeable in many styles of music. That's what made him attractive to bands like the Beastie Boys and Cypress Hill, groups that liked to experiment with different styles and weren't afraid to try something new.

In the early years, hip-hop artists relied on sampling and other pre-recorded or electric sounds to make their music. Hip-hop songs were produced by a DJ using various forms of sound equipment, not by live musicians. But innovative hip-hop artists like the Beastie Boys, always on a quest for new sounds and better music, experimented with using live musicians to record and perform their music.

While on tour with the Beastie Boys, the members of Cypress Hill saw how live musicians could contribute to hip-hop music. They were interested in working with a live percussionist, and they instantly clicked with Eric. After his tour with the Beastie Boys ended, Eric Bobo joined Cypress Hill. The crew was complete.

It seemed as though whatever Cypress Hill turned out turned platinum. But when album sales began to decrease, rumors began to spread that the end was near for the group. Rumors increased when group members began to work on their own projects. But, despite headlines that Cypress Hill was over, the group has carried on.

# Together and Apart

With Eric Bobo on board, Cypress Hill released their new album, *Cypress Hill III: Temples of Boom*, in 1995. This album was decidedly slower and darker than the previous two albums. Fans weren't sure about the music's new direction, and the album didn't sell as well as its predecessors. Nevertheless, it still went platinum.

Many people thought that the change in the music, moving to a more somber, introspective sound, reflected tensions in the group's relationship. Sen Dog was reportedly unhappy with his position in the crew, since B-Real was the lead MC. Sen, the deep, aggressive voice of the group, was essential to Cypress's overall sound. Nevertheless, he seemed to always be second in line, often coming across as B-Real's backup.

## The Albums

Soon after *Temples of Boom*, Sen Dog took a break from Cypress. He wanted to pursue a solo career and see what opportunities he'd have outside the group. He formed a band called SX-10, a rap crew with a heavy punk flavor. Being part of another group and trying to have a solo career, however, didn't end Sen Dog's affiliation with Cypress. In fact, each member of Cypress Hill wanted to have a solo career outside of the group. DJ Muggs and Eric Bobo already had vast experience producing and providing the beats for other artists, and they continued to do so while remaining members of Cypress Hill. B-Real also **collaborated** with other rappers and eventually pursued his own solo work.

Focusing on solo efforts, however, didn't leave enough time, energy, or creativity for recording another studio album right away. While the group's members explored other interests and opportunities, they looked to their previous work to keep Cypress Hill afloat. In 1996, they released an album called *Unreleased and Revamped*. Rather than having new material, it featured new takes on older material. The album was composed of tracks that hadn't made the cut for their other records and remixed songs.

By 1998, Cypress Hill's members were all back together again and ready to release their fourth studio album, appropriately named *IV*. It was their first studio album not to reach the platinum mark, but it is nevertheless reportedly DJ Muggs' favorite Cypress Hill record.

After *IV*, Cypress Hill released a flurry of albums, starting with a Spanish album, *Los Grandes Éxitos en Español*, in 1999. Most of the songs on this album were not new but had been translated into Spanish. *Skull & Bones*, their fifth studio album and their fourth to go platinum, came out in 2000. It was a double-disc set meant to showcase the band's different leanings. Rap songs were compiled on the first disc ("Skull"), and rock-oriented songs filled the second disc ("Bones").

In interviews, the group acknowledged that their journey into rock might not please everyone. After all, lots of their

Part of the fuel for rumors of the group's breakup was a perceived conflict between B-Real (shown here) and Sen Dog. Some believed that Sen was treated like B-Real's backup singer, and that the tension was too much for Cypress Hill to bear.

fans were into hardcore, gangsta rap and weren't really the rock-and-roll types. But Cypress Hill encouraged those fans to be open-minded, saying that if they didn't like the music, they could just look at "Bones" as a special collector's item. *Skull & Bones* was followed by a live album, *Live at the Fillmore*. Then came Cypress's sixth studio album, *Stoned Raiders*. It was released in 2001 and had disappointing sales. Undeterred, the group put out an EP (extended play CD) called *Stash* in 2002.

**Sen Dog decided to try his wings as a solo artist. He formed another group, but he never cut ties with Cypress Hill. Like the others, he did his own thing, but he came back to the group that was home.**

Between 1993 and 2002, the band definitely had its ups and downs, and there were times when people predicted the end of Cypress Hill. But the steady stream of releases proved that, despite ventures into solo careers, the group was still going strong. In 2002, hip-hop was hitting the greatest heights of its popularity, and Cypress Hill was still a relevant part of the culture.

# The Most Popular Music in the World

By the new millennium, hip-hop was bigger than anyone could have dreamed it would become. It was now some of the most popular music in the world. Hip-hop was the new cultural language of young people. Its fans could relate to each other even if they came from vastly different backgrounds. For perhaps the first time in history, a poor kid in the inner city was listening to the same music as an upper-class kid in Beverly Hills. It was a revolution that even spread around the world, linking fans in the United States with fans in Asia, Europe, the Middle East, and elsewhere.

Young people's love of hip-hop wasn't just about the music. It was also about the fashion. Kids across the country were wearing baggy pants, expensive running shoes, and oversized shirts. Fashion houses like Tommy Hilfiger and Ralph Lauren picked up on the trend and created hip-hop-inspired clothing lines. In turn, these labels became popular in inner cities. Middle- and upper-class youths in suburbs and the wealthiest neighborhoods wore the very same clothes as their inner-city peers. Fans were expressing their common tastes, regardless of their social background. Hip-hop was topping the charts and shaping lifestyles.

As hip-hop's popularity grew, the ever-present criticism followed suit. After the appearance of gangsta rap in the late eighties and early nineties, the disapproval surrounding hip-hop steadily increased. By 2002, the criticism was coming from all sides. Many adults criticized the youthful fashions as imitating gang members. Hardcore rappers criticized pop-hip-hop artists for "selling out." Inner-city hip-hop fans criticized wealthier fans as "posers" who had no real-life connection to or understanding of the music. And the biggest criticism, made by some parents, critics, fans, and hip-hop artists alike, was that the hardcore and gangsta styles had gone too far, making music that degraded women, glorified gangs, encouraged violence, and promoted hate and prejudice.

## Fighting the Fire

By the time Cypress Hill released *Stash*, the heat was really on, and some people dragged the group and all their albums out as evidence of everything wrong with hip-hop. More than anything else, Cypress Hill's hardcore lyrics came under fire. On every album, their lyrics focused on guns, violence, murder, and drugs, and their songs often disrespected police and authority figures.

Cypress Hill didn't see a problem with having such hardcore lyrics because they felt those lyrics were the truth—they were the reality of the ghetto and the world the group's members (and a lot of other people) had grown up in. In an interview with concertlivewire.com, Sen Dog talked about those lyrics, saying that they were about real life and they had to be hard-hitting to be legitimate. Furthermore, he said that when people listened to Cypress Hill songs and heard about the cold reality of gang life, they might think twice about pursuing that dead-end road:

> "I think you definitely got to put intelligent lyrics down. You just can't come up and rap to the beat, shuffling my feet, sound so sweet. Rhyming isn't about putting no riddles down. It's about reaching people in their [brain]. It's cool to party . . . whatever. But at all times

*you must watch your back. This is real life. This is the world out here. As easy as you can have a good time you can just get jacked [killed]. It's just that easy. You have to put some reality into your lyrics. Or else it makes no sense to be from the streets and know what you know and see what you've seen and not relate that to the people that are out there. Maybe someway change a life a little bit. Or maybe have someone think it over before they rob somebody or steal a car.*

Poverty is a problem all over the world. Hip-hop, the music that raps about the real world, has also spread worldwide. Each culture develops its own version of the genre, making the music relevant to its people.

*Nowadays, anything can get you [shot]. Even lookin' at a [woman] wrong can get you smoked. You know what I mean? You have to put that kind of reality in there."*

He went on to say that, although there were people who would insist their explicit lyrics glorified and encouraged violence, that was really not the case. He said that theory was a total misinterpretation of what their music was really trying to say:

*"We never encourage violence. If you listen to any kind of records from 'Killer Man' to 'Insane in the Membrane.' . . . Well, there's knuckleheads out there that's going to listen to it and hear what they are going to hear. And then there's those intelligent people out there that will listen to it and hear what they're going to hear. But if you listen clearly to a lot of the messages that we put in. It's not to abuse anything or to encourage anything. It's to more or less think about your overall situation. Your circumference where you stand at on this planet. Because your feet can be taken off of you at any time. Real easy! So it's more I think about recognizing your situation and make your decisions from there. I know a lot of knuckleheads, Cypress fans that take 'Kill a Man' for what they think it is to go blast on somebody. But it's all about self-defense."*

Whether people approve of it or not, hip-hop's harsher side has its roots in the grim realities of the world where it was born. Hardcore rappers tend to defend their lyrics by claiming, as Sen does, that those lyrics are just a reflection of reality. But some hardcore rap doesn't just reflect the violent reality of the streets; it glorifies it. On the other hand, behind all the profanity and violence, some hardcore rap is actually critiquing that reality, commenting on its craziness and hopelessness, and encouraging listeners to choose a different path. Cypress Hill says their songs are on this second side of the aisle. But that message isn't always crystal clear with fans. Eric Bobo backed up Sen in the interview, but also admitted that people can take their music the wrong way:

> *"It's all personal interpretation. We can write a song and have a certain interpretation. Once it's out in the public everybody is going to get their own thing about it. Like you said, some people might take it in a more offensive way. Some might take it in more defensive ways. It's not something we are trying to encourage but we realize it can happen."*

With each album, talk has increased that the end of Cypress Hill is near. Despite such doomsday comments, the guys carry on, not ready to be relegated to the pages of hip-hop history books.

# 5

## The Men and the Message

Cypress Hill has faced criticism and controversy from the beginning. They didn't let that stop them back then, and they haven't let it stop them now. In 2004, the group released their seventh studio album, *Till Death Do Us Part*, and its lyrics and themes were as gangsta, hardcore, and pro-marijuana as ever.

### Still Going Strong

Despite steadily releasing records for more than fifteen years, many people began speculating that *Till Death Do Us Part* would be Cypress Hill's last album. The group's members were by now all rap legends, but none of their later albums achieved the same sales and airplay as *Cypress Hill* and *Black Sunday*. A new generation of hip-hop artists, many of them pop-hip-hop artists, now dominated the airwaves. Gangsta rap was finally seeing a decline in popularity as more and more people came to believe that it did, in fact, contribute to the glorification and continuation of violence, prejudice, and sexism. Perhaps hip-hop culture was outgrowing the innovators of the past like Cypress Hill.

The fact that Cypress Hill's members were once again focusing more of their efforts on solo projects also fueled the rumors that the group was through. Sen Dog was still working with SX-10 and had now joined his brother, Mellow Man Ace, in a partnership they called The Reyes Brothers. In 2006, their highly anticipated album, *Ghetto Therapy,* hit the airways to positive reviews, especially for the single "Traffic."

B-Real's reputation and talent also allowed him to pursue other opportunities. He created two mixtapes, *The Gunslinger* and *The Gunslinger Volume II: Fist Full of Dollars*. He also collaborated with other artists including Busta Rhymes, House of Pain, the Dog Pound, Eminem, Wu-Tang Clan, Dr. Dre, Fear Factory, Everlast, and Ice Cube. In 2006, he teamed up with Snoop Dogg, the legendary West Coast rapper with dozens of coast-to-coast hits, in a single titled "Vato." The single was released on Snoop's eighth solo effort, *The Blue Carpet Treatment*. B-Real's first solo album, *Smoke 'n Mirrors*, is set to be released in 2007.

DJ Muggs continued his solo career as well, something he had done even while being part of Cypress Hill. He released a solo album, *Dust*, in 2003; worked on compilation albums for the Soul Assassins collective; DJed and produced for artists like House of Pain, Eminem, and Everlast; began his Sirius satellite radio show; and started his own label, Angeles Records, 2005. Like DJ Muggs, Eric Bobo also pursued his solo music working with other artists and recording his own album, which he described to latinrapper.com as "Latin Jazz tip with a bit of Hip Hop contemporary flavor."

## The Next Chapter

In 2005, Cypress Hill released *Greatest Hits From the Bong*, which didn't do much to end rumors that the band's run was done. In fact, many people saw the release of a greatest hits album as further evidence that there would be no new studio records from Cypress Hill. In an interview for latinrapper.com, however, Sen Dog said that, contrary to the popular rumors, he didn't think the 2004 release of *Til Death Do Us Part* signaled the end of Cypress Hill's music making together:

> *"Being in a group is like being in a family, we've known each other the last 20 years. Everybody has their vision of where the group should go next, I don't*

While talk of the end of Cypress Hill and gangsta rap is premature, CD sales have decreased. Some believe it's because people are fed up with the controversial lyrics. Others point to changing buying patterns. Today, rather than buy CDs, many music lovers purchase only the songs they like and download them to their mp3 players.

*think we are gonna stay away. I think Cypress will continue, I don't think* Til Death Do Us Part *will be our last album, by any means. Right now after this touring here, we'll chill and spend some time apart and see how we feel about things. I think we really need to re-invent our music, re-energize it, come out with a real . . . take no prisoners type thing. I don't see Cypress like going away, I think we're gonna come back."*

**You know you've made it big when you appear on *The Simpsons*!**

That comeback is now scheduled for release in 2007. After some time apart, Cypress Hill did indeed return to the studio together. Now their eighth studio album is on the way, and fans are anxious to see what the always-innovative crew is going to come up with next. Cypress Hill has a way of surprising people and staying relevant, even as the hip-hop world changes around them.

Throughout the group's career, Cypress Hill has changed with the times, while still keeping their music "real" and alive. It's difficult to say what the group's future work will bring or how their new music will be received. However, based on their previous albums, it seems safe to bet that their music will continue to reflect the changes in the members' lives as they get older and continue to mature.

## Changing Men in Changing Times

It seems, after nearly twenty years in the business, Cypress Hill may be adjusting some of their attitudes toward life and music making. In one interview, DJ Muggs admitted that he had to take a break from smoking pot to work on a recent album. He said he needed a clear head to let the music come through. In an interview with latinrapper.com, Sen Dog spoke similarly about calming down and cutting back for the good of his health and the music:

"When you first start touring . . . it's one [really big] party, you drink too much, smoke too much, stay up too late, and not necessarily eat good, that sort of thing. You'll burn out, that'll kill you after a while. You can party every now and then, you don't have to party every night. The better you take care of yourself, the better you'll be out there."

Sen also stated that they aren't the only ones who have changed. He says that hip-hop music and the industry have changed as well. And while he and his crew members have matured over the years, some of the changes in hip-hop aren't as positive. In the interview, he seemed to mourn the loss of a hip-hop culture that focused on social struggles and politics for a culture that glorifies fame and bling. He said that the artists of his generation were all about the message, while some of the artists today seem to be all about the money:

> *"it used to be more of a Hip Hop culture thing. It was more conscious MCs talking about building the culture, more family oriented. Now it's more materialistic, kids talking about their money in videos, showing off their jewels. It's more of a thing now, 'look at me I'm rich, I'm gonna flaunt in your face'. When I came out people were more modest, doing things for the culture. Public Enemy was talking about uplifting the black community, KRS-One was teaching kids about hip hop. It's lost that. Now its like, 'look at me I'm rich!'"*

It might come as a surprise to many to hear Sen talk about hip-hop this way. With all the hardcore lyrics and gangsta themes, Cypress Hill might not seem like the most socially concerned, value-based group around. But the crew definitely feels they have their own sense of conscience and right and wrong. In fact, in an interview with ukhh.com, B-Real said that the group is actually quite religious. They may not be your standard churchgoers, but B-Real said each member is spiritual in his own way, and that spirituality is an important part of their work:

> *"we are quite religious, cos no doubt, we wouldn't be where we are today without God on our side, we*

*pray before a show, I pray every morning. My practice though, is separate from the rest of the group, cos maybe I believe in what they don't believe in, know what I mean? I would never force it on them."*

It's just one more aspect of a group that, when one looks deeper, is far more complex than the shocking lyrics that have made them infamous. Cypress Hill believes that, at the end of the day, they will be remembered for more than profanity and gangsta themes. They hope to be remembered as musical innovators who daringly helped hip-hop become the influential culture it is today.

**Nov. 20,**
**1965**   Senen Reyes—Sen Dog—is born.

**Jan. 28,**
**1968**   Lawrence Muggerud—DJ Muggs—is born.

**Aug. 27,**
**1968**   Eric Bobo is born.

**1970s**   Hip-hop is born in the Bronx section of New York City.

**June 2,**
**1970**   Louis Freese—B-Real—is born.

**1980s**   Hip-hop enjoys crossover success.

**1986**   DJ Muggs, Sen Dog, and B-Real meet.

**1990s**   Gangsta rap becomes popular, especially on the West Coast.

**1991**   Cypress Hill releases its debut album.

**1993**   *Black Sunday* is released and immediately hits #1.

**1993**   Cypress Hill appears on *Saturday Night Live* and is banned for life after its appearance.

**1994**   The band plays at the Woodstock festival.

**1994**   *Rolling Stone* names Cypress Hill Best Rap Group.

**1995**   *III: Temples of Boom* is released, the first with Eric Bobo.

**1996** Cypress Hill performs on the "Homerpalooza" episode of *The Simpsons*.

**1999** The group releases its first Spanish-language album, *Los Grandes Éxitos en Español*.

**2000** *Skull & Bones*, the group's first double-disc project, is released.

**2005** Cypress Hill releases *Greatest Hits From the Bong*, fueling rumors that the group will disband.

**2007** Cypress Hill announces a new album.

## Albums

| | |
|---|---|
| **1991** | *Cypress Hill* |
| **1993** | *Black Sunday* |
| **1995** | *III: Temples of Boom* |
| **1996** | *Unreleased and Revamped* |
| **1998** | *IV* |
| **1999** | *Los Grandes Éxitos en Español* |
| **2000** | *Skull & Bones* |
| **2000** | *Live at the Fillmore* |
| **2001** | *Stoned Raiders* |
| **2002** | *Stash* |
| **2004** | *Till Death Do Us Part* |
| **2005** | *Greatest Hits From the Bong* |
| **2006** | *Ghetto Therapy* |

## Number-One Singles

| | |
|---|---|
| **1992** | "How I Could Just Kill a Man" |
| **1992** | "The Phuncky Feel One" |
| **1993** | "Insane in the Brain" |

## DVDs

**2001**    *Still Smokin'*

**2003**    *SmokeOut*

**2003**    *Money Power Respect*

**2004**    *Cypress Hill: The Ultimate Video Collection*

## Awards and Recognition

**1994**    *Rolling Stone* magazine: Best Rap Group

# Books

Bogdanov, Vladimir, Chris Woodstra, Steven Thomas Erlewine, and John Bush (eds.). *All Music Guide to Hip-Hop: The Definitive Guide to Rap and Hip-Hop.* San Francisco, Calif.: Backbeat Books, 2003.

Chang, Jeff. *Can't Stop Won't Stop: A History of the Hip-Hop Generation.* New York: Picador, 2005.

George, Nelson. *Hip Hop America.* New York: Penguin, 2005.

Kusek, Dave, and Gerd Leonhard. *The Future of Music: Manifesto for the Digital Music Revolution.* Boston, Mass.: Berkley Press, 2005.

Light, Alan (ed.). *The Vibe History of Hip Hop.* New York: Three Rivers Press, 1999.

Quinn, Eithne. *Nuthin' but a "G" Thang: The Culture and Commerce of Gangsta Rap.* New York: Columbia University Press, 2004.

Waters, Rosa. *Hip-Hop: A Short History.* Broomall, Pa.: Mason Crest, 2007.

Watkins, S. Craig. *Hip Hop Matters: Politics, Pop Culture, and the Struggle for the Soul of a Movement.* Boston, Mass.: Beacon Press, 2006.

Zephaniah, Benjamin. *Gangsta Rap.* New York: Bloomsbury Publishing, 2004.

# Web Sites

B-Real
www.brealonline.com

Cypress Hill
www.cypresshill.com

Cypress Hill in *Rolling Stone*
www.rollingstone.com/artists/cypresshill.com

DJ Muggs
www.djmuggs.com

Eric Bobo on My Space
www.myspace.com/ericboboofcypresshill

# Glossary

*blues*— A style of music that developed from African American folk songs in the early twentieth century, characterized by sad songs often played over a repeating harmony.

*collaborated*—Worked with someone to create a project.

*crossover*—A work that becomes popular in a category other than the one in which it originated.

*cutting*—Manually queuing up duplicate copies of the same record in order to repeatedly play the same passage.

*demo*—A recording made for promotional purposes.

*ethnic*—Relating to a person or group who share a national, racial, linguistic, or religious heritage.

*funk*—A type of popular music that blends jazz, blues, and soul, and is characterized by a heavy rhythm bass and backbeat.

*innovative*—Taking a new and original approach to something.

*innovators*—Individuals who introduce new ways of doing things.

*jazz*—Popular music that originated among black people of New Orleans in the late nineteenth century, characterized by syncopated rhythms and improvisation.

**mainstream**—The ideas, actions, and values that are most widely accepted by a group or society.

**notorious**—Well known for some undesirable feature or action.

**platinum**—A designation indicating that a recording has sold one million units.

**punk**—Fast, loud rock music often containing confrontational lyrics.

**samples**—Piece of recorded sound or musical phrases taken from existing recordings.

# Index

## About the Author

MaryJo Lemmens is a children's nonfiction writer who lives in Toronto, Ontario, Canada's largest city. Before moving to Toronto, she lived in the United States and South Africa. She received her bachelor's degree from Smith College in Northampton, Massachusetts. She has written numerous publications for young people.

## Picture Credits

Corbis: front cover, p. 2
Cypress Hill: p. 46
Hatcher, Chris / PR Photos: p. 39
Fox: p. 50
iStockphoto: pp. 32
     Ambrits, Tamás: p. 49
     Deshaies, Julie: p. 16
     Heshem, Karim: p. 8
     Lombard, Shaun: p. 15
     O'Driscoll, Christopher: p. 31
     Pruitt, Mark: p. 12
     Rashap, Dmitriy: p. 22
     Shaughnessy, McKevin: p. 43
     Valentin, Wilson: p. 11
PR Photos: pp. 24, 28, 36, 40

To the best knowledge of the publisher, all other images are in the public domain. If any image has been inadvertently uncredited, please notify Harding House Publishing Service, Vestal, New York 13850, so that rectification can be made for future printings.